Abandoned Gardens

Alice Kavounas

Abandoned Gardens

Selected and New Poems
1995-2016

Shearsman Books

First published in the United Kingdom in 2017 by
Shearsman Books
50 Westons Hill Drive
Emersons Green
BRISTOL
BS16 7DF

Shearsman Books Ltd Registered Office
30–31 St. James Place, Mangotsfield, Bristol BS16 9JB
(this address not for correspondence)

www.shearsman.com

ISBN 978-1-84861-536-6

For permission to print the first two stanzas and the final stanza from the
George Seferis poem, 'The Return of the Exile', we thank Mrs Anna Londou,
acting for the Estate of George Seferis.

Translation of George Seferis's 'The Return of the Exile'
copyright © Rex Warner, 1960.

Poems printed here previously appeared in the following publications:

The Invited (London: Sinclair Stevenson, 1995)
Ornament of Asia (Exeter: Shearsman Books, 2009)
Thin Ice (Bristol: Shearsman Books, 2013)

The author thanks the editors of the following publications in which various of
these selected and new poems have initially appeared:
*Acumen, Bananas, London Magazine, London Review of Books, Magma, New
England Review, Open to the Weather, Out of Fashion: An Anthology of Poems,
Permanence: Porthmeor Studios, Poetry Book Society Winter Supplement,
Poetry London, The Long Islander, The Times Literary Supplement.*

The Return of the Exile

George Seferis

'Old friend, what are you looking for?
After those many years abroad you come
With images you tended
Under foreign skies
Far away from your own land.'

'I look for my old garden;
The trees come only to my waist,
The hills seem low as terraces;
Yet when I was a child
I played there on the grass
Underneath great shadows
And used to run across the slopes
For hours and hours, breathless.'

[…]

'Now I hear nothing,—not a sound.
My last friend too has sunk and gone.
How strange it is, this levelling
All around from time to time:
They pass and mow here
Thousands of scythe-bearing chariots.'

from *Poems,* by George Seferis,
translated from the Greek by Rex Warner
(London: The Bodley Head, 1960)

*To all the people who have been forced to leave their homeland,
especially the children.*

Contents

from THIN ICE

PICASSO'S BICYCLE

from

The Invited

(1995)

Scenic Wonders

i
I'm falling the full mile
to the floor of the Grand Canyon

where earth hits bottom, and walls measure years
inch by inch

like the marks a mother makes
above her children's heads.

ii

The dream continues. I appear amid
the tangle of life supported by a forest floor.

The silent mattress of pine needles
is threaded by invisible snakes. As I stage

my own brief scenes of comic relief, perform magical
transformations of character and sex,

something in this classic haunt
of children's nightmares and real life

seduction is beginning to tear me
limb from limb...

iii

But the dream continues. I'm in strange waters,
taking sounding of the ocean floor.

Warped ridges rise to meet me
as I float face down to the depths, finally

eye to eye with the grains of sand that stick
and separate like the buds of a parched tongue

when it cleaves to the roof of a mouth.
The waves of terror

don't wake me—now I'm falling through floor after floor
numbers flashing past. The dream continues.

Riverside Drive

All day the river
flows past the living room mirror.
We dip in and out
breathing normally.
During dinner
the sun slips behind the mirror.
Later, we clear the table
fishing out the knives and forks.
The river runs to black.

First light. The living room mirror
wakes the opalescent river.

Birthday Visit

Every step betrays him:
he's old now, and bent against the wind,
the Sunday Times billowing in his arms
like an unwieldy spinnaker
towing him down icy streets.
He won't see me
as he completes his small journey,
carrying home news of a world
he no longer inhabits.

I think he's thinking of the days he meandered home
through olive groves and orchards
his mandolin tucked beneath his elbow;
where Sundays passed in sunshine
and young men danced their dances
in the shade.

It's too late
to try to catch him.
I've lost my father
in his father's orchard.

Cutchogue, Long Island

The fields are being burned tonight,
well before harvest.
The road to the sea
is a river of tar, impassable.
That rock, that rock. Worn down
beyond recognition; the smallest wave
swallows it whole. Even the sunset
is not what it was:
its fires banked; while small
animals search for the glow
of a camp-fire (the kiss,
the whispered conversation) up and down the furrows
that lead, flaming, to the shuttered summer house.

1133 Park Avenue

Every door was closed.
The blinds were taut against the sun
and the children all in place
except the son they'd had to send away.

The mother lay
in a room at the back of the house
knowing it no longer mattered,
chain-smoking,
flipping through the fashion magazines
and listening
to the hum of the air conditioner.

It fell to the eldest daughter
to turn it off.
Sweating slightly in her tennis whites,
she opened all the blinds
on the day her mother died.

Abandoned Gardens

i

Like a migrant pair
who'd regained the homing instinct
you touched down
on littorals you'd resisted for so long.

Indigenous diphthongs, consonants and cadence…
Instead of lapping at your inner ear, or flowing
back and forth for forty married years
hollowing out a tideless, inland sea,

the lively cries of your native tongue
began to break over both of you; syllables
slapping you on the back—*Kalos orisate!**
Each face you looked into resembled your own.

* * *

Americanised, camouflaged in the dull plumage of drip dries,
you felt strong enough to untwist certain Athenian alleys.
But old intimacies have their underside; to go home
is to walk barefoot over miles and miles of krokalia**…

Here in the bleached city of ma's childhood,
she readied herself to visit her dead. Stray cats
kept rubbing up against her bare ankles
like a litter of insistent memories. And you, Da,

sat and gauged the distance between now and then.
Sipping at the scaling coffees of your youth,
you planned how to navigate—without drowning—
the whirlpools of the wine-dark past.

ii

After slipping through the Turkish nets
(catching kith and kin), this had been your first refuge.

'Birthplace of democracy!' a foreign city,
none too friendly to a stowaway of peasant stock,

even one whose language, after all, was Greek.
Still, you'd survived that rite of passage

and before migrating further, you'd perched here.
A world war and two children later,

you were returning
to see what was left of your father's lands.

Would those figs and olives still be fattening in the sun,
melons ripening on foreign vines?

iii

The sensitive coast will remain closed to all visitors.

Operation Attila came as a reprieve. You meandered,
pretending interest in rocks and broken columns,
gazing impatiently at eyeless gods,
stumbling over the cool heads of toppled warriors.
Old quarrels made a mockery of your plans.
That rusting cargo of thoughts you'd hoped, at last,
to unshoulder in Anatolia, dragged at you daily.

You were just killing time, your and your Penelope,
the pattern of your journey unravelling.
You felt no itch to wander: Corinth, Delphi, Mycenae;
what of those ill-fated families, unanswered oracles?
The air was full of riddles.

iv

The sensitive coast remained closed.
It's as if that's what you'd always been, everywhere:
a visitor and once more, unwelcome.

Holed up again in America, that odyssey a failure,
the present began floating beyond your grasp.
Did the towers of Manhattan become your Byzantium?

How you flew! Circling high above the Aegean,
ordinary objects became unreadable,
the faces of your American-born children a blur.

None of us could reach you in those last years.
You'd escaped from an adopted country to your Aivali,
those childhood orchards, the one sustaining memory.

v

I'm left holding your long-expired passport.
Freeze-framed and flash-frozen,
your frightened face stares out from that limbo
shared by travellers and exiles.

'Date of birth.' Mis-recorded indelibly in ink.
Some lazy, low-level American immigration officer!
We joined in that conspiracy, celebrating
shamelessly his slip of the pen, clapping each year

as you blew out more candles… Yours alien's fear
of detection was unreasonable then. I understand it now.
It saddens me, like your meant-to-be-amusing story
about our made-up name, the centre-piece of family lore.

* * *

'A boy came bearing fruit each day
from his father's orchards. His teacher,
Ottoman to the core,
regarded gifts from Greeks with pleasure.
He dubbed the boy *Kavun*,
according to the fruit, namely melon, which he bore.
Gradually, *Kavun* clung as naturally on a Turkish tongue
as honey on the back of a spoon,
and *Dracoulis* was allowed to wither, syllable by syllable,
like fruit in suddenly abandoned gardens.'

Where are these orchards of your childhood, Da,
where our Greek name still echoes among the stones?

vi

As melon upon melon from our orchards
surrendered into Turkish hands,
as the soil grew even rockier,
was Dracoulis beguiled by the Empire
or beguiling? Did he ever sigh, *What's in a name?*
then quickly curse, cross himself and mutter
Nothing, or *Nothing much*? Relinquishing his patronymic
freed his sons to flourish
so that wherever those tendrils chanced
they'd persist, somehow, as tenaciously as vines
watered at the roots with fear
in the hot-house of borrowed time.

A Narrow Passage

The cat chokes
on her fur. The hooked fish

completes its final curve.
Summer heaves into the city

closing off possibilities.
My mother

prises open the lid
of my father's eye, a web of burst capillaries,

cross-hatched—like those rag doll stitches
that track across his scalp.

I take my mother's arm from his, and tug
her down the corridor. She steals

a backward glance at the steel crib,
and his hand, fallen through the bars.

Monday Evening, London

A child in her flannel nightdress
is being hugged; and in another window
someone is peeling potatoes, then crossing
to check the oven. Guests will soon arrive.

A couple sits comfortably. She tucks
her leg beneath her. He folds the paper.
I lip read their small talk.

The Man in the Lacoste Shirt

America has pinked your cheeks.
The lines that hem your eyes reveal
nothing but laughter.
Years of tennis have taught you how to grip
another man's hand without flinching.
And you're a prime example of the lean
expensive cuts
that don't marble the flesh.

It's taken you nearly fifty years
of crossing borders
to reach this bed
to annex this dark-haired
olive-skinned
slash American, living
in another country.

You could drown in your own innocence.
The alligators basking in your bedroom closet
will emerge each night
to clasp you with their scaly tails
while you stand naked
in a pool of Connecticut moonlight.

Hydra

I've come to collect the lemons.
The square is empty. This morning
I looked for you
in the church at Rafina.

I borrowed flame, lit the wick, spoke your name.
I didn't expect miracles.

A woman approached,
speaking as if I were a tourist.
I'm wearing three sweaters, she said,
despite the sun. In another life

she could have been my mother.
The cat slid into the shade. The square
shone. The woman walked away. I lit
another cigarette and thought of stealing

a single lemon from one of three trees.
The fourth was the pine shading the cat.

Later, I'll walk down the narrow steps
to the edge of the harbour. I'll order coffee
and eye the painted eyes
on the old men's boats.

Athenian Night

Three orderlies stand folding sheets
over an empty bed.

An in a small room
off the garage,
alongside a ramp where frozen sides of beef
come hurtling down,
lies a man.

Only his feet are visible,
the body too tall
for the winding sheet.
Still warm and finely veined,
his feet are evidence of the freshness of his death.
It is as if he had thrust them out
from beneath the sheets
seeking cool relief in the small hours
of an ordinary Athenian night.
Not to prevent us from mourning the wrong body,
not as the flawless end of a man
whose feet are all we have to go by…

Not that it isn't enough. He knew we would find him
alone in this unholy room with its makeshift altar
of unlit Coke-bottle-candles
and no one to speak his name
so quickly had they wound the sheet round
his arms, chest, legs, eyes, mouth, head
all but his feet,
guileless, unanointed, unmoving, unmistakable.

And I imagine in each of them a hole pierced
that he might rise, just for a moment, from the dead.

Fugue

My mother's flesh
has lost its affinity
for the bone. Her eyes,
which once, I imagine,
flickered prettily
over the rims of crystal goblets,
stare now with longing
and stored disappointment.

Her pianist's hands
tremble with disease
but her voice hardly falters
as she embellishes
the short, familiar subjects
which neither my brother nor I
can take up or develop.

Whispering Wordsworth

I still see a scarecrow
ignoring klaxons
recklessly crossing Syntagma Square
to embrace me.

Mother's sister in my childhood dress
lost in my sleeveless mustard yellow
with the white ric-rac—
all colour wrung from you.

'God will protect us!' You were
a crackling cough,
mirror of a mirror, Mother's
death mask and, in time,
mine. Your tubercular pallor,
made near-lethal
by mustard-yellow, was my first whiff
of the aftermath of war.

If only you'd found a silken thread
within the cardboard boxes of simple cottons
mother sent year after year
to lead you out, inch by inch, from the ruins,
from that cramped attic to Long Island summer days.

You forgave Jesus
everything, and this was your reward—
to be eased out of life whispering Wordsworth.
And here's the inevitable hand-me-down
of memory: mustard yellow tempered
with rows and rows of ric-
rac. Mustard yellow. Rows and rows of bright
white ric-rac.

False July

The electric light tangles the stems of the carnations.
They're slow to open.
Outside, my garden darkens
in the cathedral chill of Sunday afternoon.

Five o'clock. I sit out the slow hour,
white, tight-fisted
like the buds that resist this false July.

Easier for the tulip; it enters—
crimson, bowing deeply in the heat—
overweening and satiny and feverishly seeking applause.

After Veronika Voss

I walk along its cobbled back.
I know no one. The street, reptilian
in the night, is giving off exhalations
that hang, uncertain, in the lights.

I pass massive wooden doors,
each a faded frontispiece of Europe.
I've been given a name, a number: *'Is this where
Dr Katz...?'* Upstairs, the rooms are far too white.

I hold my breath. No one could leave
her mark here. Like a fetid garland
my breath begins to seep out
through slightly parted lips
into the sterilising air. It hangs briefly,
then disappears. Dr Katz enters.

'The palm is painted white,'
I comment. *'Is it dead
or perfect?'* She walks past the plant
to the window. *'Do you have a view?'*
I persist, pretending calm.

'It's only glass,' she explains,
*'that separates us from the next room.
And we have boiled eggs for breakfast
every day.'* If I stayed,

I'd spoon the soft yolks whole into my mouth,
let them slide back a bit and squeeze
them with the fat of my tongue
until they broke and ran down my throat—
their thick, thick yellow.

But I say nothing. *'The couple downstairs,'*
Dr Katz continues, *'are dying.*
Tomorrow, we'll join them for tea.' Their skin
was like crumpled velvet and they took
the pills that she gave them
with honey. The number tattooed blue
on his left forearm
was still fresh. I'll discover
all this too late. Tonight I imagined
I was only a visitor.

The Invited

This seasoned, polished wood
was, to me, as thick
as speech. All the hours we spent
around this table; I, the invited,

hovering on its perimeter.
Raw, dull-witted, downcast,
sober—in bad shape, generally. Stealing
fire from the two of you; grasping slowly

the sense of things beyond me.
How you two
never noticed anything apart from each other
continues to amaze each of us.

Your glorious indifference. It gave me
the licence, each time, to return.

The Visitor

A rib-cage; shoulder blades
too sharp for comfort; skeletal arms
and legs; a skein of hair, a half-
expectant stare. She is, now,

like a visitor to a large museum
who has entered from a snowbound city street
and slowly removed her scarf, hat, gloves, coat,
even her husband's thick Mexican sweater.

She stands, holding her garments
as if they no longer belonged to her.
Uncertain, unable to move, she decides

to check them, receives in exchange
a plastic tag in the low numbers.
Unencumbered, she floats, mute,
into the main exhibit.

Cheyenne

Eventually, even the most worldly traveller arrives
somewhere. He's been away
so long he can no longer remember
when or why he left. This is the farthest
he's ever ventured; it's off all the maps he began with.
Outside, just beyond the silos, herd of cattle
float on ancient grasslands. He's beginning to feel
the altitude. Someone hands him a key.

'When the two of us
turn our keys within a certain number of seconds,
what is called the Launch Vote
is sent out.'

The keys look like ordinary front door keys.

He walks the length of the corridor.
The doors are marked
in ways known only to the management.
He tries every keyhole.
This fresh turning and turning
revives him slightly.

'It takes two Launch Votes to launch a missile.'

These four walls. Has he come this far
simply to enter another room? There's no view—
he flicks on the TV. Broken.
He looks around for a phone.

'So it requires two separate crews,
one in another capsule
with all four of us turning keys within
a certain number of seconds.'

If he could press a few buttons, talk,
tell someone he's here.

There are no buttons
to press, just keys to be turned. The keys
look like ordinary front door keys.

Nuclear Family

And for their dog
his wife buys meat in bulk,
dividing it, re-dividing it.

Each morning, someone—his daughter?—
perhaps his younger son—is detailed
to search out their evening meal.
A carefully wrapped parcel hits the counter.
It thaws so slowly.

The children return from school,
play with the dog, attempt their homework.
Everyone listens for father's car
as they begin to eat their dinner.

He's nowhere near them.
I had him a sock, his watch: *'Is that the time?'*
But there's no rush. He begins describing the battalions
of tinned soups and tuna; stores of cereals and roots;
the height and depth of their deep-freeze, the steaks:
'We could last out a nuclear winter,'
he concedes, fishing for his car keys.

Walking out from Batworthy Farm

We stood in the centre of the stone circle
conjuring up a wedding (not ours)
and other rituals. We imagined the difficulties
of transporting the priest—gasped at the state

of the guests' hair, the hatless best man.
And before the groom could say 'I do!'—
the bridal veil blew halfway across the moor.

* * *

Sunday couples straggle across the moor,
making their weekly pilgrimage, hand in hand,
shouldering backpacks, to witness what?

The sky, perhaps; a stream; the distant Tor?
These found stones; a congregation of sheep?

The Lizard

Black tongue of land
languishing in the mouth of Coverack
lapped at by pre-dawn
small-fisted waves.

a lull in birdsong—
that gap in nature's soundtrack

Dredged from bleary seas
a haul of Celtic gold
coins the day. Hour after hour
the gods gamble away
their morning's plunder.
Its value alters hourly—
brash as base metal by noon.
Locals avoid its whitened eye
hanging above them like a buzzard
fixing on invisible prey.

* * *

The day's sovereign
burnished by wind, thin as a hunter watch,
slides down the far side
of my unconquered afternoon
scouring the vast, cloud-filled pocket of blue.
The printing of shadows resumes.
The sea's uneven surface
reveals another day's
spilled currency; false light
trickling over watery ridges.
Waves conveying nothing
while fishermen trawl deep.

As the sea drinks in
the last of the earth's light
I watch a silver hammock
rise amidst these blackening trees.
The ancient coin
melting into the distant hedge
glows as scarlet as the berries
clinging to the common hawthorn
which scratches at its disappearing face.
Slowly, another night breathes out
settling on my shoulders its sequinned shawl.

Swallowing the Sea

1

'Πέφτω. "Ολο πέφτω.'
Falling? You keep falling, mother? How weightless
the verb is in Greek, twisting towards earth—
'a sere leaf'—it would be easier to regard you
as a figure of speech. Instead, I worry
at the rubbery spirals of the telephone cord
like an old Greek thumbing his beads.

Not that we haven't always talked like this,
your native tongue in counterpoint to mine.
Oh, your failed attempts at subtlety: 'It's nothing, dear,
nothing serious. I don't go out. I fall
right here, here around the house.'

Remember Madame Gautier? 'Stand!' I'd plead—
a five-year-old girl-general
faced with her porcelain smile; my doll,
kid-booted and splendidly outfitted,
kept toppling off my shelf. I'd rearrange
her fragile limbs, and scold her
as she took another spill. You'll break,
you'll suffocate! Or so I thought, rescuing her
once more. Trapped in her brilliant taffeta
Madame kept parachuting to the floor.

'Don't worry. Your aunt is here
to lift me up. She's much better now,
thank God!' The pair of you. No, not dolls
exactly; more a species of bird, peculiar in its habit,
teetering around, sadly overbred;
holed up and isolated in fashionable Connecticut.

'I keep forgetting, dear—'. Your memory
is as sharp as mine. *What? Forgetting what?*
'To tell the doctor. You know,
about my falling all the time.' *Your apartment—*
jagged with possessions. It's a bad line.
Our goodbyes get drowned in static.

2

My dog's at my elbow. I grab his lead
and slam the door. *So why tell me?*

As if I didn't know. Three thousand miles
from your clutter and still it finds a way
to wash up here. The light on this stretch of coast
is harder today, and last night's storms have emptied
the sea's stomach. There, on blackened sand,

a haul of fish. Like quicksilver my dog is on it. Pure animus,
he clamps a jelly-eyed trophy between his stone white teeth
and takes off down the beach. That tangy fish, inch by
skeletal inch—inhaled like an ocean breeze.

A moist clump of feathers
snares my foot. This time I'm prepared.
I yank him off the splayed dead gull
and snap him on the lead.

That freakish bone disease
has clenched your spine, mother—your shoulder blades—
sprung like damaged wings.

3

Keeping my dog close, I skirt the pile of slime and guts
and quickly back track. My guilt deepens,
snagging now on torn ribs of ships—smashed like toys

and stashed in the watery attic shadowed by the Manacles.
Divers know they're there. I've looped the braided leather
loosely on my wrist. *Telephone the doctor, please.*

The neon nets are hopelessly tangled; the fissures
in the rocks form pools: a doll, dismembered,
plays among the seaweed. *The healing salt wind,*
how it shivers through his fur—my dog,
still on the run, swallowing an ocean whole.

Winter Migrants

A morning wind, thumb-printing the skin of the sea.
Crossing the driftline I surprise sanderlings, dunlins,
knots—they rise and twist—a snow that won't settle.

Fresh hieroglyphs of winter migrants mark
the white-throated beach. My footprints follow me. Above,
the rigorous tamarisk-fringed path keeps going.

A spill of rock. Utterance of gulls.
Standing here at the recurring lip of the world
I turn out my pockets for words; find sand.

Cape Fear

Exhausted from my walk, I come across
a bench, and taking it in at a glance,
decide to slide

well along its narrow planks
to give these nailed words
air: 'A sailor who loved

Richmond Park.' No date inscribed
no donor named. Who knows who gave
this land-locked sailor leave?

Floating freely
across his deer-strewn acres, untroubled,
riding at anchor in the emerald depths

of the rhododendrons, at last
to circumnavigate the world with ease.
Even now (with the wind kicking up)

he sails as steady as this bench. *To know
you've rounded it*: Cape Fear
no longer clouding your horizon.

Home Ground

for Fred

Our friends are reversing down the drive.
Waiting in the warmth of our front door
we wave until they shift and disappear down the lane,
city-bound. As a child, bundled back and forth,

how I longed to feel like this,
slowly taking root, inconspicuous as moss,
right as rain. However hard I smiled
at my lucky country friends,
captured like wild-eyed young deer in our brights,
I couldn't take their place. Stuck in the back seat,
invisible, wishing in the dark that we could stay—
but nothing could arrest Dad's Oldsmobile, I knew that.

Now, standing here with you, on home ground
darkness surrounds me like family.
Had I known, all those years ago (but how could I)
that one day I'd be here, those journeys would've been
more than counting miles… Precisely not to know
is to be a child, watching the rain streaming on glass,
and to be always looking back at the shrinking past
through the oval window that tells you nothing new…
Not to know that one day I'd come home; that these lanes
would lead simply to my front door, to find me moored here
next to you in the naked country night.

from

Ornament of Asia

(2009)

The Road to Ithaca

To deliver his first-born to college
he drove north to Ithaca on icy roads
facing down the one-eyed beams of snow-plows
in our big-toothed, second-hand Buick
that leaked oil, forcing us to stop
every half-hour to top up—
in bitter, wind-chill-factor weather.

Born and raised just south of Troy, amidst
Mediterranean breezes and donkeys,
my Ottoman Greek father's annual trip
must have reminded him of other journeys,
other herculean tasks he'd tackled.
But he was no Trojan warrior, no Greek
hero, just a man trying to hold his own

in America, where no one interferes—
not even when your car lets you down.
Oncoming drivers are as snow-blind as you!
My father's odyssey was repeated
every year, until my brother's graduation.
Now Ithaca has become my metaphor:
breaking down in winter, then journeying on.

On Seeing the Statue of Liberty for the Second Time

As the tallest girl, I got to play the Statue of Liberty.
On the night, I walked on stage, raised one arm
and stood stock still, crowned, in my sickly green
costume which the teacher called 'verdigris',
our old living room curtains actually,
which my mother had sewn and draped just so.

I was proud to be the famous Statue
to hold high the familiar torch—
a flashlight concealed in cardboard.
But after an hour of holding it
straight-elbowed, well above my head
that paper cone had turned to lead.

So when it came round for me to recite:
'Give me your tired, your poor, your huddled…'
I, too, was yearning, (a verb I'd just learned),
to be free. At last, I understood the words
which I'd rehearsed. Now I sympathised with
those poor folks who'd entered New York harbour;
who, on seeing the Statue of Liberty,
were about to shed whatever burdens
they'd shouldered in their homeland.
And after their arduous sea journey,
were they ever on the brink of giving up?
Suddenly my co-star, playing Uncle Sam,
broke my train of thought, grabbing me boldly
by the (other) hand to take our bows.

Foreign-looking in that crowd, whispering
in their embarrassing language,
and applauding with the rest, were Mom and Dad.
I smiled, welcoming them to my country.

Aivali

This neck of sea
swift running
is where you crossed
to escape a death
more certain than
the heat of the mid-day
sun as it beats down
on this stretch of beach
where I stand and peer
at the coast opposite
searching for a sign
an indication of some sort
the flicker of an oar
a tell-tale rhythmic plash
of a prow cutting through
these Aegean straits
a sign to let me know
that somehow you sense
my presence decades later
as I grasp, at last,
what you had to go through
that night to flee
with your brothers
from Aivali
to reach this shore
with nothing left
but your lives
held onto as tightly
as the oars
in your clenched fists.
The necklace of lights
opposite in Ayvalik
comes on
yet what I see

is your Aivali. I recall
every sweet memory of it
you still held—
how your eyes would shine
as, time and again,
you'd describe to me
your long-vanished life:
Mother, father, brothers
and your band of friends—
young men playing mandolins,
making music on a Sunday
in your family's orchards of
quince, fig, peach
and plum… all ripe
for the gathering.

Fall Weekends — I

You were hellbent on burning the brilliant
freshly-fallen ones, mingling with
the crumpled millions that must have dropped
for years before you'd set foot here
decomposing into a thick humus
more akin to earth than leaf; slow to flare up.

How could I have known that you were elsewhere
on those crisp weekends, raking up the past,
feeding insatiable fires—from Anatolia
to the tip of Long Island. You stood there,
transplanted, like a sturdy tree yourself;
I never thought to ask
what you could see as you stirred the embers.

Fall Weekends — II

Before you was a pyramid of fire
burning day and night. As we'd go off
to play, you'd stay put, raking over
that same ground year after year,
clearing layer on layer of detritus
alone, with just the birds for company.
And, of course, your trees.
Was there a memory of another fire
rising through those leaves; your beloved
Smyrna ablaze, burning before your eyes?
You seemed content—or was it resigned—
to clear the plot of land that belonged to you,
while contemplating your narrow escape.

Before me burns this image: you, amidst
your tall North American trees, tending
that unending pyre of fallen leaves,
the fire speaking to a fire inside you.
That much I know.

Everything Is Before You

Before you is your city, burning to the ground.
Before you stands a friend who'll never be found.

Before you, the farm you were born and raised on.
Before you, the orchards, their fruit long-since gone.

Before you, your mother. She will fall to the knife.
Before you, a rowboat that will save your life.

Before you, your brothers, each wielding an oar.
Before you, safe harbour on the opposite shore.

Before you, the woman whose hand you take.
Before you are woods to clear, and cultivate.

Before you, a catalogue of mutual slaughter;
the birth of a son, then a daughter.

Before me, the earth that conceals the truth.
Before me, a portrait, the vestige of your youth.

Ornament of Asia

What if, on a day in mid-September,
I awoke as usual to this idyllic view—
a crescent of a bay—but instead of Coverack
it's my father's city, Smyrna, nineteen twenty-two,
her harbour thick with battleships flying flags
from the world's so-called fair-minded countries.

Would I sense the danger on that brisk wind?
Would I try to leave? And if I panicked
what, besides the children, should I grab?
Would I abandon everything—even
the carefully tended fig, coming into fruit.
Would I be swayed by wild rumours...

mounted men are heading toward the city
set to sack and burn it... Or would I chance it
and stay, thinking, we've made our lives here
for thousands of years, trading in and out
of this city. Flee? Flee to where? How?
Look at the ships. They must be here to save us,
I would have thought. Would I have thought that?

And like as not, I might have rushed the children
through the stumbling crowds, fled from the 'safety'
of our house. I'd have joined the floods of people
edging toward the harbour, that numbed procession
with no exit plan, pushing for a place
on the last steamer, to get themselves out,
to go anywhere. Anywhere but here.

What if we plunged into the sea and swam
toward those smartly dressed crews—French, Italian,
British, American—on board, standing watch—

surely they'll see us coming! We're swimming
for our lives, stroking the water like it's the last thing
we will love… But wait—-some crews are throwing back
the swimmers like small fish… we see them drowning,
drowning within inches of those foreign hulls.

We dog-paddle back to shore, breathless, trapped
between fire and the sea. The ships' masters declare neutrality.
Who would have us now, orphans of the 20th century:
Armenians… Jews… Ottoman Greeks… Palestinians…
exiled on the wrong side of history.

The Red Sofa

II

Their mother is diligent. She skips nothing, not even Deuteronomy, although none of it is very clear to any of them. There are scores of names, and puzzling events occurring in mysterious places.

For a long time, the children can grasp only the rhythm of the remote language. It soon becomes as ingrained as the classical music they hear their mother playing, and the music on the radio.

These two languages, musical and Biblical, eventually interlace, imparting to the children a vast sense of complicated and immensely beautiful sadness. That the world is a bewildering place, becomes a familiar notion.

The native Greek accent of both mother and father is stubborn. They continue to converse in Greek. Luckily for the little girl, her older brother has taught her English from the start, and they speak to each other only in this language.

Both children are always at the top of the class. Their parents will soon come to expect this. Throughout their school years they know they must perform brilliantly.

Flags

We walked south on 6th, against the traffic,
toward a column of sky, brand new, blank and blue—
a vacuum—funnelling us all the way downtown.
We stopped at the lights—a well-dressed woman
throwing up into a wire bin—the lights changed.

The next day, I would go to an exhibition,
see Gaugin's woodcut, Mahna no Varva Ino—
and think back to that woman
punctuating our journey toward what
will always be known now as Ground Zero:
once just a coda to these unremarkable streets
where my mother filed away her final years;
and where (all those decades ago) father earned our keep
travelling here by subway, in starched white shirt,
suit and tie, braving the drenching summer heat.

The makeshift kiosks were busy selling tat—
baseball-style FDNY hats; postcards
of then and now; framed photos of destruction;
homely items to pin to the railings that ring the cemetery.

There, opposite: the infamous plot,
vast enough to have housed a civilisation.
We joined the slowly moving crowd
and walked silently round and round…
What could I leave here—a sandal, a ring?

I saw children's indigo handprints
on a giant canvas; the hieroglyphs
of a thousand signatures; news clippings
honouring a son or daughter—the ink

already fading—heroes and heroines
in their hometown papers; banners from schools;
a love letter to a lost husband.

And, like pilgrims who offered up their rags
at ancient wells for St Audrey to heal their ills,
people in their thousands had draped their T-shirts—
torn, rain-soaked—flags flapping in the hot wind.

The Red Sofa

Every evening, each child takes turns to practice the piano for precisely one hour. Their mother supervises their progress, her perfect pitch detecting a wrongly played note, even within a complex chord, from any room in the small apartment.

Their mother teaches them for the first six years, and when they each turn twelve their instruction is taken over by a Mrs Rose from the prestigious Juilliard School of Music. She's plump and friendly. Lessons are at her home, an apartment only slightly larger than theirs, and Mr Rose always arrives toward the end of the girl's lesson. He busies himself until the hour ends.

Mr Rose plays jazz and the girl longs to hear him but is too embarrassed to ask. Or even to ask Mrs Rose to ask. The couple laugh together and have no children.

Neither the girl nor her brother is brilliant at piano, and at sixteen they will stop taking lessons.

Their mother, an accomplished pianist whose debut concert in Athens was at age nine, attempts to prevent this from happening.

She informs Mrs Rose that she will try everything.

The Red Sofa

V

The mother allows her son to put aside Beethoven's lengthy 'Moonlight Sonata' in favour of a piece of sheet music the boy bought with his pocket money. "Davy Crockett."

She instructs Mrs Rose to proceed with it.

This experiment with a popular tune is a brief flirtation, however, which merely prolongs the boy's lessons for a few uneasy weeks and underlines his mother's keen disappointment. He never plays the piano again.

Four years later, the girl, having mastered Beethoven's 'Pathétique', simply stops. Learning to play jazz, or turning to the violin, appeals to her. But she knows that nothing would ever be considered an appropriate substitute for the piano, and so never discusses these options with Mrs Rose, nor with her mother.

Meanwhile, the mother consoles herself with the knowledge that both children excel at school.

Their father seems entirely unmoved by these musical events. He is proud of his wife's extraordinary talent, but has never touched the keys of their immense black piano himself. Nor has he selected a record from his wife's modest collection, placed it on the gramophone, and settled into the sofa to listen.

At least not to anyone's knowledge.

Paperweights

Sunday, Feb 16th, 1941:
In the wild grey water after last week's turmoil.

A few weeks after she entered those words
Virginia Woolf walked out one afternoon
into that terrible water, toward no island
no distant shore, river-walking, offering herself
up to the elements. Standing knee-deep,
unable to go deeper, she slipped into the shallows
of the Ouse, words and all, weighed
down, weighed down, lying prone in the stone-filled
grave of her, without a splash to toll her death.

This was no accident. Before setting off
she'd left a letter, carefully composed.
As I walk along the beach, I imagine her
stopping and bending, bending and pocketing,
bending and pocketing… or had she been hoarding
those lethal stones all along? Had she dared,
even, to place them, just so, on her desk?
And had anyone asked, paperweights,
she might have whispered. Paperweights.

The Red Sofa

VI

One winter evening, the family travels into Manhattan to hear the mother play the piano accompaniment for a classical singer who is performing at Carnegie Recital Hall.

Although they own a rather fine car, a grey, solemn, second-hand Oldsmobile, they find themselves taking the subway.

As soon as they descend into the familiar, cindery, fluorescent gloom of the underground, the girl is struck by the wild incongruity, in that setting, of her mother's glamorous evening gown: a full-length, peacock green taffeta which her mother has to grab hold of with both hands in a great bunch to prevent it from blackening with soot.

The girl longs to escape. But she stays close, and the four of them, like a flock of peculiar migrant birds who follow a prescribed, if demanding route, alight and perch, one by one, on the steps of the down escalator.

Her mother continues to hold the billowing folds of her evening gown, now with one hand, the other fixed firmly on the rubber banister to steady herself, in case the hem catches in the fast-moving mechanism, and plunges her headlong to her death.

Lunch in Ayvalik Harbour, Anatolia

Frankly, we chose the one that looked expensive,
figuring the waiters would be polite,

older—speak more than restaurant English.
They might even know Greek. I could ask

about the past, show them the photograph.
It was just an outside chance, but still…

The linen is pink. Impeccable.
Silently, they bring bread, water, olives,

plate after plate of meze as we watch
boys slither and splash in the harbour—

diving, but not for coins, just larking about.
They look like brothers, cousins. I can't help

studying their faces for a trace of my father,
his brothers. My brother, me.

The couple at the next table toss bits of bread
into the sea—minnows arrow toward each morsel

like metal shards to a magnet. Our octopus arrives,
glistening in the local olive oil, tentacles diced bite-size.

Jalem… Sinbad… Jalem… Sinbad… small boats
moored inches from our table, rock gently,

cradling young fishermen who sit mending
tangled nets. When we've eaten our fill,

we begin to stroll along the front. The boys
have gone. I give the place a backward glance.

The waiters are attacking their own late lunch.
I've come this far, yet asked them nothing.

La Sarrasine

for Linda

Flowerless oleanders, an olive tree
unpruned, a brave geranium or two—La Sarrasine
left to you, suddenly, in mid-winter.

How the details of death have absorbed you… tired
from arranging food and flowers for the mourners
you stand, like this house, rudderless, in the teeth of the Mistral.

At last, you allow yourself a moment,
here in the garden, to breathe. Bracing yourself,
you invite me to follow your gaze… Together

we stare out across the vineyards—that vast
and familiar valley of carefully tended vines,
row, upon row, upon row, shorn of fruit,

each clipped close to its roots—and then beyond
to the seasonless backdrop of pine-dark mountains
where, come the Spring, you plan to return

to scatter your father's ashes. There, you explain,
there they will join your belle-mère's,
which you scattered only last Spring.

Last night…

the banging of the neighbour's shutter
rattled through room after room after room… who
will come after us? And then

who? And then? This cold
country, warmed by a hot sun,
now holds you.

* * *

Sunday. The giant cloche tilts sharply
calling the faithful to church. The flowers
you left by the altar have already begun to fade.

Go quickly—single out the bright ones—
fill a jug with water,
arrange them as best you can.

Now walk carefully up the stairs
and place them next to
what was your parents' bed.

The Red Sofa

VII

The up escalator, running opposite them, is lined with grey or navy-suited men returning home from work. The girl acknowledges their stares; this is what it's like when a movie star mixes with ordinary people. She pretends not to be embarrassed, neither for herself nor for her mother.

The concert hall is full. Seats have been reserved for them near the front, on the left side so that they can see their mother's hands on the keys. The piano music and the singer begin.

Within minutes the father is seized by a fit of coughing which forces him to rush from his seat and steal up the aisle toward the exit sign. Eventually, having missed most of the concert, he returns and sits quietly.

The mother, as usual, plays fluently. Later, they all go next door to The Russian Tea Room and order expensive French desserts.

Neither the girl nor her brother breathes a word of the incident, but it's clear that their mother already knows who it was who ran up the aisle coughing. She doesn't seem angry.

They have an excitingly late night, returning in the empty subway carriage to Queens.

Pastoral Scene (after Samuel Palmer)

The harvest moon rises in blood
over the shorn fields. The golden sheaves
stand like ancient stone works.
Winter lies ahead. These endless fields
of stubble are hard on children
without good shoes to their name
without someone to carry them through.

Letter to a Garden

You are time well spent, making a frond-like
fist of every kind of weather, drawing water
up through your throaty tap root—
sharing it—giving permission for native
bulbs, unruly weeds, plant hunters' seeds,
to germinate into this poet's palette:
Calla Lily white, bruised reds, forget-me-not
blues, Mexican yellow, Himalayan pink,
seven shades of green.
With the wind hard at your back,
you shelter the less hardy of us:
winter jasmine, the lenten rose, peonies.

Listen to the birds in your hair!
Another spring. You are time itself.

Lure

The sea tilted toward me like a painting.
I could hang it from a hook in the sky.
No one about. A boat too far out
to see me. The water is high-tide-deep.
Unthinkable to plunge in. Unthinkable not to.

Two Chairs

If I were sitting in this chair, with you
alongside in this identical one,
both of us leaning slightly forward
facing the dancing fire as we talked,
knowing that the fire was also dancing
on the polished floorboards, that all of it—
two chairs, our backs, the fire—was reflected
in the shimmer of the living room mirror,
this winter evening might have been one
to recall, perhaps mention, years from now
in a memoir. As it is, both chairs are empty.
The mirror has blackened. You are lost;
I am busy dismantling the house: books,
walls, floor—all of it consumed by fire.

Open to the Weather

In this, our fifth winter,
storms lasso the house.
A distant sea wall
buckles. The trains falter.
Telephones die.

Our sand-rich beach blackens
with weed and rock from God
knows where, and the tide
rises... stealing summer land.
The world becomes water.

I dress carefully and walk
full face into a Force 9... crossing

the first field; the second;
at the third stile my dog

refuses. We are wind-whipped and
sodden. Go back, he pleads,
his head cocked in the direction
of home. Let's go back. That night

the roar of the chimney-wind peaks
and I hear you mutter in your sleep:
I can't take it

anymore. I can't
take it anymore.

* * *

The morning will be bright. Silent. The sea
will resolve into its cat's eye green,

the storm debris mustachioed with cream.
That clay pot we placed in the shallow cleft

on the far terrace will not have shifted
an inch, as if it were the hollowed out

eye of the now-spent storm. Our dog will sleep
his morning sleep in the winter-thin

shadow of the granite balustrade
with the wind's shaping hand ruffling his dreams.

Suitcases

Let's pack now, put our weekend selves into
these smart suitcases—you in this one,
me in that—and head out toward the tip of the Island
where sea spray gave the glorious old Inn its name.

We've packed clothes to play in, to swim in,
as if we're still children, though I know
you were not one of those whose parents
brought them here. This place holds nothing for you.

When your mother speaks with her neighbour from Lvov
you leave the room. You cannot stand the repetition
of their talk of suitcases, of packing, of leaving
everything; of her struggles to bring you up in Brooklyn;

of how lucky you are. Of how she misses her husband.
You cannot stand feeling lucky, even as we walk
along this oceanic landscape, the salt wind
scouring our city selves, giving us respite before we pack.

Years later, I stand where the white-shingled Sea Spray stood.
I knew that a mysterious fire, one winter night, had demolished it,
yet to see for myself this long stretch of beach, unbuilt, unpeopled...
Nothing, I know, compared to the emptiness of Lvov.

The Red Sofa

XII

The girl, no longer a girl, again moves abroad. She takes only her favourite clothes and books.

And for many years, the sofa, still in red velvet, is lodged in a huge warehouse somewhere in New Jersey.

She lives in a succession of flats and houses, and sits on countless sofas, none of them her own.

So many of them are faded, and even slightly torn, especially in the grandest rooms, and she wishes her mother could sit alongside her now to see how relaxing it might have been to cherish her unprepossessing sofa; to accept, even in the most superficial ways, the passing of time.

After five years, this transplanted daughter has all her things sent to her. Some things she had forgotten she owned.

And in a house which she imagines she has settled into, she installs the resplendent red sofa which she occasionally naps on, warmed by pale winter sunlight, the book she is reading slipping from her grasp as the sentences run together.

So Soon, So Soon

for Fred

One word at a time, I'll begin losing
what I know of the world, forgetting first
the name of a friend, or the cove we used to
walk toward; things you'll quickly fill in for me.

Then, linking a string of words will be beyond me.
Half-formed sentences will pile up like stalled cars
rusting beneath snow. As bright days dissolve into
purple afternoons, flurries will keep swirling upward
past the closed window, long into the night.

And when whole chapters have receded,
you'll recall them for me with a word—seems like yesterday,
I'll whisper. Here, on my pulse, I plan to write
your name. Mine's already on this tight white
bracelet, last name first—as if I could forget that!
Or where I am now, and so soon, so soon.

A Writer's Beach

An exultation of larks… murmuration
of starlings… a garrulousness of gulls?
As I follow the lip of froth, sea birds
by the dozen lift off, only to resettle
further down the beach, nestling in the sand
like warm-blooded stones: an artist's installation.
Amidst their screaming conviviality,
I note the feathers that mark their passage:

a long curving grey, a dainty white comma,
and this—a downy, chocolate brown—each find
a perfect quill. Clearly, what brings me here
isn't simply the white-lipped waves beneath
ink-splattered skies, but these birds, oceanic
birds on the wing—each lending me a pen.

from

Thin Ice

(2013)

Seal Harbor, Maine

You must have slowed your step for me
and stooped slightly, to reach my hand.
I'm three, against your fit and weathered
fifty-three—old, in that America, for a father.

On our walks, sea met primordial rock—
crashing, ebbing, slithering through fissures
into rock pools: my mirror-bright worlds. Later, freewheeling
gulls would make off with the remains of lobster lunches.

Postcards kept arriving—close friends, cousins, colleagues,
your brother, living through the death throes of civil war.
Your already depleted country, still fighting with itself.
Here, it was croquet and iced lemonade

on the sloping lawns of the silvered clapboard mansion
whose owners had befriended you and mother. And I had
the run of it! Seal Harbor, affording you a break—
shelter from feverish heat, squalls, of that summer of '48.

Thin Ice

The man who twirled me round each Saturday,
older than my brother, younger than my father,
was called Otto, a name like no other
within my circle of school-friends; family.

Tall, thin, thin-haired, blond, his face a long pale
oval tilted skyward, chin thrust forward,
Otto carved elegant, contiguous figure-eights
at a languid pace across this pristine,
miniature landscape of man-made ice,
in his weekly attempt to teach me

how to skate. As his pupil, I was, frankly,
something of a disappointment to us both,
not that Otto nor I ever let on
to mother. I'd attempt, but never master,
the art of skating backward, nor learn to glide
as he did, hands clasped nonchalantly

at the small of his narrow back, dreaming
perhaps, of more graceful dancing partners,
of Austria, who knows? Otto's English
remained as vestigial as my father's:

Left foot, lift now! Now! Turn, spin. No, no, no.
At Christmas, in the shadow of a giant spruce,
we'd celebrate with hot chocolate, topped
mit swirls and twirls of *Schlag*, pale Austrian-
American Otto, and Greek-American me.

On thin ice, glistening at Manhattan's heart,
we skated round and round each other,
ringed by Rockefeller's millions, Otto's
flashing blades describing dazzling figure-eights;
mine, increasingly imperfect zeroes.

Villa Mokoras

In the demolishing heat, we read and mostly sleep away
the afternoons, on one or another of the stone terraces
where coils of fat yellow hose await the gardener's hand
to unwind and flick, unwind and flick
unleashing cool fresh water to quench the countless *pithoi*
festooned with hibiscus, oleander, geraniums—
scarlet blazing against blazing skies. Through half-lidded eyes,
I glimpse how, at intervals, he slowly raises the silver arc
of braided water, and by dipping his head toward the mouth
of the uncoiled garden snake, slakes his own unending thirst.

Hair-Trigger

You were new at work, ridiculously
handsome, though your close-cropped hair was ice-white.
It had turned, you said, practically overnight—
you and your friend were fighting side by side

when he folded at your feet, shot dead.
We'd only just met. But I stayed the night—
woke to the sight of you springing to the front
door at a sound I barely heard—was it

the elevator reaching your floor—your neighbour
coming home in the small hours? You'd reached
for something tucked under your pillow like a charm—
then leapt out of your side of the bed, returning

minutes later holding a gun. I listened
as you tried to explain how it was with you,
while I thought how it would be. Even in
your own apartment, you were on a hair-trigger.

In time, it will go back to your own colour,
the doctor had promised—jet black before
Vietnam. At dawn, I crept silently out of bed,
felt your eyes on me as I dressed quickly, and left.

Helter Skelter

In the freezing hold, hurled helter skelter
into the dark, lie our clothes, neatly folded,
entombed in cases, the arms of jackets and sweaters
crossed loosely at the wrists, or pinned back—

fragile blouses rubbing up against fresh shirts—
buttoned up to their necks—silk ties tightly
coiled, leather shoes buffed and stuffed
under their tongues with balled up socks,

or handfuls of jewels stashed in their toes;
trouser legs all bent double—all of it travelling
in parallel, our baggage always with us,
flying blind, shadowing every journey.

We reach our destination, pluck our possessions
from the revolving belt—nearly identical cases
concealing nearly identical possessions. Later,
we unpack, unfolding and smoothing each

precisely-creased garment as if to smooth our own
stiffened arms and legs. We slip into our second skins,
check the mirror image of ourselves, and venture out
helter skelter, into the jumbled day.

High Summer, The Lizard

The wind is shivering the broad back of our neighbour's field. I walk along
Its bumpy spine, this narrow tamped-down path that snakes through
The barley undulating on either side of me. I'm swimming
More than walking, or afloat in a small boat, my hand trailing idly,
A five-fingered comb, luxuriating in this sea of miniature plaits, each
Impossibly perfect, waving on its slender stem, *en masse*
A magical assembly of shiny schoolgirls with their neatly-plaited hair,
Appearing to greet me on this August morning. I head toward the far corner
Of the field, the stile a knuckle of old stones placed just so: one, two, three,
Jump!
The wind at my back. Ahead, the path through another shimmering field.

Neon-Green Man

Maybe he knows something. A bomb. What if
he's planted it. Under a seat. My seat.
The neon-green man's on the run, guarding
the exits. So far, no one's questioning him.

I could yell *Stop! Thief!* if he were a common criminal,
and hope for the best. But maybe he's just an ordinary guy
who's caught the Norovirus. He's so green, as if he's about
to throw up. Or, as if he's been swimming in chlorine.

That could be it. An illegal Chinese immigrant—
in his head, still escaping from some factory—
poisoned from years of making jeans like these.
If that's true, I'll rip them off! Never buy them again.

On the other hand, the man doesn't look Chinese.
What if the theatre's on fire? While I nipped out
to get sweets, did I miss something? An important
announcement? What if he's that terrorist—you know—

Chemical Ali—this neon man is green, after all. No,
can't be him. Ali Hassan al-Mahid's been caught.
Hung. This faceless man—could he be Kurdish?—a lucky
survivor, blinded by chemicals? He seems to appear

everywhere, yet running in place. Running and running
all over London. If he's running from bush fires—
in his head, I mean—if he's Australian, running from bush fires,
that's really sad? But smart. That's probably why he was saved.

The official Australian advice has just changed:
Don't stay in your house. Run. Run for your life.
Your house isn't safe. Your house is fuel.
Did you just feel a shudder? The imminent earthquake.

It's scheduled to occur anytime now;
definitely within the next two hundred years.
You say it's too late? Have all the men
turned green and I've only just noticed—

now when the lights are dimming, and the show's
about to begin? Should we stand up, follow
this transparent man who's green to the marrow—
or run like hell in the opposite direction?

Should we wait for further instructions
in silence, together, in the dying light?
I'm staring at the sign. What do you think?
What exactly does this glowing man know?

My Arboretum
VALLIER

PALM   *Tracycarpus fortunei*

Scissor-fingered fronds
fan out against sea and sky.
A fresh show of hands.

PLUM   *Prunus domestica*

Espaliered, burdened
with fruit—ovoid, split, oozing.
The wasps' *déjeuner*.

CRAB APPLE   *Malus x billieri*

Scarlet ornaments
hang from every wet black bough.
Christmas in July.

MYRTLE   *Myrtus communis*

Depthless evergreen
set alight by summer's white.
Winter will follow.

TREE FERN   *Dicksonia Antarctica*

Its Queen's wave greets each
invisible, passing breeze.
It thrills to fine rain.

FIG   *Ficus carica Moraceae*

'I don't care a fig'
is hardly my view of figs.
A blackbird's delight.

OLIVE   *Olea europaea*

Pliant branches arch
then dip, from wind-twisted trunks.
Weave me crowns of peace.

Requiem Mass

The Benedictine Father isn't above the sharing of a small joke—a pleasantry—
as if to say, yes, I'm a man of God but tolerant of life on earth; of how and why

you, and you, might stray. He outlines the well-trodden path to salvation
open to late-comers to the faith; early defectors. The Father leaves us

in no doubt as to his belief: the body in that coffin isn't dead, as in finished,
decaying. Soul extinguished. He talks of heaven, of where that coffined-body

will go to be resurrected, to become one with mind and soul. It sounds as if
we, too, must believe heaven is a place, with much better weather than here

on this chilly afternoon. Somewhere glorious, like the South of France
in June, without the traffic; or within a gated community on an unmapped

Caribbean island: 'Here, drink this—take of my blood. Eat—take of my body,'
intones the Benedictine Father, according to scripture. Each believer partakes

of the sacrament as the choir sings *Alleluia, Alleluia, I am the living bread*
which came down from heaven, says the Lord. If anyone eats of this bread

he will live forever. Alleluia. Yet, I stay fixed in my pew. *Lord in your mercy.*
Hear our prayer, responds the congregation. *Commune with Christ, our saviour,*

invites the Benedictine Father, in exchange, basically, for eternal life.
It's an incredible deal! Yet I don't move. Would I, in this paradise, hear music

as heavenly as the Fauré *In Paradisium* that I'm hearing now? What of books?
Conversation? No need, I guess, for a pen, or even a crust of bread

if we're to exist incorporeally (*if anyone eats of this bread he will live forever*)
until, of course, the day of judgment, when those redeemed are resurrected.

Love, eternal love—this is the currency. But, my love, will I find you up there?
Could we, in the meantime, live on air? We're being told now to look up—

'Let your thought be on things above,' wrote St Paul to the Colossians,
'not on the things that are on the earth'. Later, as they lower you, inch

by inch into the receiving earth, freshly dug, I try, try to look up. Air.
Eons of air. I will play music, pick up my pen, try to look up; to prepare.

Castles in the Air:

Porthmeor Studios, St. Ives

It begins with a line, cast into the deep.
    You sell what you catch
        and paint in your sleep.

It begins with a line, in your mind's eye.
    I'll do this and not that,
        live here, and not there.

It begins with a line, drawn in the sand.
    You're that child again
        building castles in the air.

It begins with a line, sketched onto board.
    What you know is the sea,
        you paint what you know.

It begins with a line, as wide as your brush.
    You load it with colour
        straight from the tin.

It begins with a line, infinite as a wave.
    You'll make it your own
        as you ride it home.

It begins with a line, left by high tide.
    You eye the horizon,
        life on the margins.

It begins with a line, where sea becomes sky.
    You drink in that light
        till the day you die.

It will end with a line, inscribed in stone.
    We're each moved to make marks,
        who can say why?

Picasso's Bicycle

(2016)

Picasso's Bicycle

My words aren't new. Not one.
They're re-purposed. Used and reused.
Forgive me if you've heard them all before—
perhaps in contexts more auspicious.

If you've used some of them, you'll know
each word, in and of itself, is worth nothing.
Or everything!—depending.
Depending on the word. The context. The p.o.v.

Think of a word as kindling.
Love—*I love
you*—or as a missing leg
of a chair. Broken.

So that leg is valuable. Try to find it.
One of these words could prove
to be a missing word—a leg up, *haha*,
on a brilliant idea.

Or a new phrase. New poem. Yours?
Mine. I scavenge the world,
the world of words, and like today's artists, I re-
purpose them—as artists have always done.

'Guess how I made the bull's head?'
Picasso asked his visitor, Brassaï.
'One day, in a pile of objects
all jumbled up together, I found

an old bicycle seat next to
a rusty set of handlebars.
In a flash,' Picasso said,
'they joined together in my head'.

So ask yourself, what's joining in your head right now?

'All I did', Picasso added somewhat modestly,
'was weld them together'.
But he was hardly modest.
Picasso was bold. A genius! There's a word,
difficult to re-purpose. I know you will,
you scavenger, you.

Calligraphy

New to teaching, I've been made aware
that my listening face in one-to-one tutorials
expresses disapproval, disappointment, even before
we begin our session. Understandably, this unsettles

the less confident student, and since I feel
nothing of the sort, and cannot begin to explain
to someone at least thirty years younger,
that as you age, form and content disengage,

I've taken to practising my smile as I drive to college,
checking, every so often, in my rear-view mirror
to gauge my progress. Whereas the fluent calligraphy
of a young face is more likely to reflect

the emotion behind it, the older one gets, the more
a series of punctuation marks clutters your face:
first an apostrophe, then double quotations
corner each eye. Graceful commas that once

bracketed the lips, deepen, depressing any hint of a grin—
as if a pen with indelible ink is out to re-write you.
Your once-clear face, a calligraphic disaster!
The smile I've nearly perfected

is a kind of half-smile, non-judgmental, allowing, I sense,
the students more freedom of expression. Do they know
I'm aiming for the half-smile of a kore,
those Greek 5th century BCE statues of maidens

who stare out at us in marble or wood, with a knowing look,
about which we know so little? Some say this *archaic smile*
meant the person was alive. Good news! Moreover,
in excellent health. Another view, one that I favour the most,

holds that this famous archaic smile reveals
a young woman *full of the purest metaphysical good humour…*
timelessly intelligent and timelessly amused'. With this in mind,
I start another day's tutorials, sporting my (ancient) half-smile.

Tickets for the Opera

He walked in, flushed with confidence.
A raise? New job? She smiled, waiting

for his important news: *I love you.*
He wasn't smiling.

As his words reshaped themselves
mid-air, he repeated gently,

I'm leaving you…
Tonight, he added, twisting the knife.

A new voice entered their living room.
She guessed it must be hers—

Stay, stay, until I get used to the idea.
Until, you're sure.

He'd been sure for months.
I can stay. Only until Monday.

We have tickets.
Tickets, for the opera.

Leave now! she managed.
No sound emerged.

       .   .   .

They spent the whole of that weekend
un-spooling their marriage, picking

through the debris. Was she hoping
to turn up a jewel or two?

Turn things
around? Or was she just afraid.

. . .

Monday. They left the house
together for the last time, as if

this were an ordinary morning
and they, an ordinary couple,

which now, she knew,
they were.

. . .

That night, sitting up late with a book,
she kept picturing the soprano,

alone on stage,
her mouth forming a huge 'O'

emitting unearthly sounds,
piercing the air with high notes,

the audience dumbstruck, sitting
in the dark; silent,

longing for the interval.

. . .

Later, there would be
thunderous applause.

She imagined herself
mingling with the audience

pouring out of the Opera House
into the fresh, cold air.

Riverside Drive 1973

And every night, walking
those six long blocks

home from the subway
I'd lace my front door keys

their teeth freshly
sharpened—one, two,

three, through my fingers—
the tip of each shank pointing

outward, my metalled-fist
bunched, bare-knuckled

jammed in the dark
of my coat pocket

as I breasted icy winds
coming off the Hudson.

Caribbean Christmas with Friends

Pounding surf. Three locals,
or was it four?—they multiplied
in the glare as they materialised
on the un-peopled, pristine beach.

The men brushed past us in unsmiling
silence, and just as we
resumed breathing, they turned and
faced us—blocking the way back to our jeep.

Their long knives, each held out
like a handshake,
glittered in the too-hot sun.
Cameras, watches, rings, money—

even your sister's St Christopher's medal—
patron saint of travellers…
We gave them everything
in exchange for letting us live.

You'd been silent for weeks,
distracted; busy, you kept telling me,
(and so I told myself).
On my way to Heathrow

I learned, *en passant*
you'd been seeing someone else.
You didn't know? My good friend, mortified—
but English—as confident as you

that this needn't spoil Christmas.
She stopped me from stopping our cab—
jumping out into the M4—
returning home.

You'd all assumed
I was smart enough
to realise
our affair was over.

How was I to know
the English way of doing things
is to say nothing.
Do nothing.

The men let us go. In the stunned hours
and days that followed, I stopped thinking
about you, me. None of it mattered. It was,
after all, an unforgettable Christmas—

the cab ride, the pristine beach,
glittering knives; you sleeping
in the ironing room,
alone. The long flight home.

Ocean

i.m. Apostolos Kavounas

He'd swing me up and onto his shoulders, his steadying hands
holding my ankles, so I could gain a commanding view
as we met each oncoming wave, the sea breaking against his legs,
fine spray tickling my toes. Further and further out we went,

well out of my depth, the sparkling ocean crashing around us.
Exhilarated, I drank the air, tasted salt while he stood planted—
a bronze colossus, my much older cousin, legs like pillars, sand
swirling around his ankles, sea girdling his waist, chest, shoulders,
his body easily withstanding the Atlantic's push
and pull—more than a match for its fierce undertow.

Later, I'd learn how the Colossus of Rhodes
broke at the knees after standing astride that island's harbour
for fifty years. Struck by an earthquake. Or so the story goes—who
knows? At fifty, cancer took my cousin out from under us.

The bleak basement of an Athens hospital: a body stretched out
on a pallet, swathed in a twist of sheet. It could have been anybody.
Head covered. Face, chest, legs—covered. But the makeshift shroud,
too short, exposed his ankles—bare, uncrossed, unmistakable.
And deep within him lay, I knew, his smoke-scoured lungs. The ocean
heaved him up; my drowned colossus, beached by the outgoing tide.

Maen Eglos, Lizard Peninsula

Held in the dazzling gaze of the sun's noon eye
this vast uneasy sea moves at the wind's whim,
waves cresting ceaselessly, pronouncing again and again
in a frenzy of exultation, the mile-long presence
of *Maen Eglos*, treacherous, half-hidden graveyard,
ships and souls all going down, down, hundreds
year upon year, drowning within sight of St Keverne's
octagonal spire: daymark of his burial ground, daymark of hers.

Who Will Read the Runes?

i.m. Charles Thomas (26 April 1928–7 April 2016)

for Jessica

Who will read the runes, decipher who we were
now that you're no longer?
His reading of the tombs,
mere scratchings on the stones,
served as beacons: ᚲ Kenaz. This rune helps you
open to who you are, leads you out of darkness,
allows light to enter. He was by your side
for over sixty years. Where to go from here?

Who am I without you? Together, you possessed
the gift of harmony in relationships: ᚷ Gebo,
unity with your higher self, and all around you.
This cannot be reversed.

Quickly. Carve it into a small flat stone.
Wear this as an amulet. Now. Always.

Earthscapes: The Lizard

Abandoned Quarry
Sun electrifies
the wind's configurations
on the man-made lake.

South West Coast Path
That the earth rotates
as I walk along the path,
defies all logic.

Lowland Point
We stop for coffee
on this oceanic crust:
rare ophiolite.

Asparagus Island
At half-tide, the sea,
tunnelling along a fault,
sucksinand b e ll o w s.

Kynance Cove
Only at low tide
can I confront Steeple Rock.
The Bishop stands watch.

Saint Keverne
Hooded figures. Rain.
Rows and rows of wet green stalks.
Daffodil money.

Maen Dale

The pony looks up:
you again!—and shakes his mane.
I flick mine, drive on.

Goonhilly Earth Station

i

We're tracking Tim Peake
as he defies gravity.
Five goons graze nearby.

ii

Major Peak's first meal:
bacon sandwich. We share it.
One day, pigs might fly.

iii

The door won't open.
No one panics, openly.
Open sesame!

King Harry

We drive through the dark, snaking along rain-soaked lanes,
thickly wooded on either side, the final downhill twist of road
delivering us suddenly to the landing.
White horses in our headlights.

Shuddering toward us, steadied by chains in the strong current,
weaving within its prescribed route, mastering winter winds,
King Harry eases into place, metal tongue meeting dry land—just.
We drive onto the ramp, up onto the ferry, followed by no one.

We stand on deck, the only passengers this Boxing Day night,
as King Harry carves a serpentine path, returning from the Roseland
across choppy waters, navigating the Fal's depths,
held by its chains from escaping downstream, down the Carrick Roads,
while we, like a couple of drunken sailors, get pitched to the left and right,
ferried homeward in lit magnificence.

The Wait

Suddenly, he was summoned. In the eyes
of the latest authorities, it was decided
Shostakovich had over-reached himself,
catapulting from protected, national treasure
to unpredictable liability. The call coincided
with the loss of his friend and patron,
Chief of Staff Mikhail Tukhachevsky, (no angel),
purged, aged forty-four, blamed for losing
Warsaw. Perhaps he'd over-reached himself.

When Shostakovich got the call, he thought
he knew the three possible outcomes, all of them
death, in one way or another.
Imprisonment. The gulag. Shot on the spot.
On arrival, Shostakovich was shown into a room,
told to wait. Half an hour passed. No one appeared.
An hour. Two. Two and a half hours. Three. At last
a clerk entered: 'Who is it you are waiting for?'
Shostakovich said a name. The clerk shrugged: 'Go!
He no longer works here. He was shot some days ago.'

Later, son Maxim spoke of his father's music:
'It was like a mirror of our time, and we can
recognize and understand how difficult
the years, the minutes, the hours were'.

All of a Sudden

All of a sudden I've become
frightened of death. There.
I've written it down, in pencil,
admittedly. I've spoken the words

only to myself, in an undertone,
but over and over to see if repetition
could help to diffuse their fire. To see
if they'd lose some of their gathering power.

Instead, they're gaining a certain momentum,
becoming louder. The letters of each word
seem larger, boldface as I score over them
in ink. My fault. I thought the ink might drown

their meaning. They stare out of the page—
a dare—tempting me to erase them.
Too late of course, now that I've over-written them
indelibly in ink. Now these words are writing me,

> *all of a sud den*
> *I've be come*
> *fright ened*
> *of death*

and with each passing month,
each of these syllables, twelve in all,
weighs on my mind, each one a stone
I carry with no small amount of care

to the close of the year,
in my deepening pockets.

Wide-Eyed

In my line of sight: a needle,
fine enough to insinuate itself into an eyelid,

snaking its way along the curvature
piercing as it goes, releasing—one, two, three—

anaesthetising stings—four, five, six—
an implacable wasp—seven, eight, nine

numbing my eyelid's scrap of flesh—ten, eleven
twelve -- the epicentre of this theatre.

Act I begins: the consulting surgeon
announces she will now flip my eyelid

inside out. She, and her even younger
second-in-command, plus two nurses, cluster

in and out of my narrow field of vision—
four pairs of hands and eyes hover—adept

disembodied fingers flip my eyelid, as announced.
Act II. 'Scissors, please.' I sense a snipping

along the hemispherical crease: snip and tuck,
snip and tuck, and soon enough another

needle, this one threaded with a length of filament
looping in a graceful arc, directly crossing

my line of sight. I feel a lifting of my lid—
someone is making miniscule adjustments

as if to a pesky blind, raising it, lowering it, millimetre
by millimetre to match its pair: 'Look up, look down,

look up, look down, now follow my finger—
left, right, scissors please!' The surgeon's cool

hazel eyes approach mine; her eyelids pink, taut
and delicate, unscathed, perfect as the smooth

inside of a seashell... I try to imagine the sea. The crisp
sounds of thread being snipped, snipped, snipped—

or is it my flesh? I do exactly as I'm told, lie still, silent,
alert, cocooned in three blankets, wrapped in my

blue plastic shroud, at last no longer shivering. I force
myself to focus on the giant ceiling fixture at the theatre's

far end, with its metallic sheen and six glistening
oval sections. It's unlit, if indeed it is a light.

It resembles a platter of monstrous oysters
exposed, shucked; I'm stretched out, a patient

upon a table, but un-etherised, waiting
not to be served up—but worked on—

clack, clack—various small metal instruments
jostle on a nearly table, just out of sight. Is this the interval

or are we nearing the end of this performance?
Suddenly it hardly matters. I've been quickened all into verb,

pure verb, by a needle fine enough to insinuate itself into
an eyelid. I'm helped to step down from the operating table,

cyclopean now, my sewn eyelid seen to, and bandaged,
and by tomorrow, wide-eyed, ready to receive the light.

Caul Bearer

To be born within a caul—a veiled birth, one in eighty thousand—
is to arrive in a gossamer embrace, a veil of tears, some call it

but when this veil ensnares you
dropping out of nowhere, you become a kind of caul bearer

time-travelling back to being born, not in a glistening membrane
but in a shroud, suffocating, robbed of speech, undone

by this envelopment, separated from yourself, looking out
as if through a glass, darkly. Hoodwinked,

you might say, yes, like the falcon, deceived into thinking
night has fallen as the falconer drops a hood

over the raptor's head, hoodwinking it into imagining
it's now safe to release its prey from powerful talons.

When I, at last, release my hold,
it will be in broad daylight,

like committing an audacious bank robbery
and I will not be hoodwinked,

but nonetheless caught: branded
both villain and victim, red-handed.

Pinsssssssss

The air seems tuned to a new frequency
no one else hears, as far as I know. Others

hear various sounds but we are all on
different frequencies indescribable to each other.

Silence, blessed silence is splitting wide open now
and as I enter an envelope of air, I hear it resonating as it

sssssssssssssssssssssssssssssssssssssssssplits
open, hissing stereophonically, snakelike

pressing deep into the well of my inner ear.

Unseen metallic instruments form
an orchestra without musicians. They are playing me.

The air is pin-sharp, with pinssssssssssssssssssssss
performing in unison at a pitch well above what my dog hears

as far as I know.
Perhaps the air has always been singing, as far as I know

sssssssssssssssssssssssssssssssss
sssssssssssssssssinging

in unison unison unison unison unisssssssssssssson
but in unison with what? The sound itself is not ear-splitting.

It's far more insidious. Hisssssssing, as I said, snakelike
with an invisibility I don't like.

Do I split the air as I walk? Am I just another a tuning fork
for this new music of the spheres?

For the life of me, each time I enter a room,
I cannot hear

a pin

drop.

None of It Matters All of It Matters

None of it matters

None of it

None of

it matters, all of it

matters

all

all of

 it

matters

All of it none of it all of it none of it all of it none of it
matters it matters it matters.

The Emperor's Experiment (I)

No one dared
disagree with him. And anyway,

no one knew the answer
to this vexing ancient question:

Coming out of the body, who are we?

He went ahead with his experiment,
ordered that an ordinary man,

a prisoner, be further imprisoned,
placed in a wooden barrel

into which a small hole was bored.
His plan was this: the unfortunate man

left to die, would be closely observed
particularly during the last days

of his ordeal. As he breathed
his dying breath, would his soul

separate from his wasted body,
show itself at last, in plain sight,

a living soul, taking flight? Would it
escape at breath-taking speed

from the barrel's tiny aperture,
to which was glued the eye

of the wide-eyed questioner,
Holy Roman Emperor Frederick II?

The soul resisted all experiments,
its final resting place

at one with the prisoner's body:
starved, unknowable, unseen.

The Emperor's Experiment (II)

What word first unfurled
from your infant tongue?

What if no one
had ever spoken to you,

if you'd never heard a single word
as you grew from newborn

to toddler? Is there
an ancient scroll

of a long-forgotten language
waiting *in situ* to be refreshed,

brought to light all-of-a-piece
by a brain untouched by contemporary

sounds, pristine, serene, engulfed
in silence? Hebrew, Greek,

Latin, Arabic, whatever
language Adam and Eve

whispered in, when they
stood in the garden, tantalised,

considering the merits of
biting into the apple?

Could their language be
embedded in our DNA

needing no interplay of speech
no mirroring of a mother's lips

no echo of the sound of 'no',
nor the bark of a dog. Or even 'hello'.

Would no clue emerge in the prattling babble,
the opening notes of a baby boy or girl?

Is there a language intrinsic to human life,
natural to a newborn, however isolated?

The man who had mastered
no fewer than five languages

demanded the answer. He ordered
the deprivation from several infants

of any human voice or sound
to determine whether, indeed, Hebrew

was the language God had instilled
in Adam and Eve. Unsurprisingly,

the children's health soon
 deteriorated. Moreover, they had no speech.

Children 'could not live without clappings of the hands,
and gestures, and gladness of countenance,

and blandishments', according to the
13th century Chronicle of Salimbêne.

The multilingual man, Holy Roman Emperor
Frederick II, had 'laboured in vain'

concluded the dutiful Salimbêne.
In what would later be labelled

'The Forbidden Experiment'
the Emperor had discovered nothing.

Nothing comes from nothing. Often, less than nothing,
while the value of prattle and babble continues unabated.

Tether Me

Tether me to earth with a child

      not necessarily one of my own, so I can witness joy.

Tether me with birdsong to the skies

      so I can fly for miles, return home unerringly.

Tether me to this short life with your lips on mine

      one life-long kiss, you know who you are.

Tether me to truth with rainbows

      revealing the heart of light, splitting it apart.

Tether me to the now with nettles

      a fistful of stings hidden in the tall grass.

Tether me to the sea with a shell clasped at my ear

      as if I could fathom the distant shore.

Tether me.

               Let me go.

Will o' the Wisp and What the Wind said

Something about leaves dancing in circles
at October's end, as if once again
the year's chasing its tail, and how children
from good homes, dressed as witches and urchins,
take to walking wet streets at dusk, shadowed
by ghosts of lost children (fairies, spirits)
undisguised; see them approach in the half-light
knock-knocking on glossy front doors, house after
house, face to face with scoured-out pumpkins,
triangular eyes, jagged-tooth mouths—
heady with fire, lit from within, white magic
burning for this night only; jack-o'-lanterns
soon left to rot, elf fire, the 'foolish fire',
ignis fatuus, extinguished by drenching rain,
each pulped face discarded like a bundle of sticks,
deluding all who chase the will o' the wisp.

Neither trick nor treat, says the wind to no one
in particular, the following day,
as children in their ordinary clothes
kick at the leaves dancing in circles, circles.

On Reflection

Upside down trees. Sunken forests. Full moon
in a pond. Before anyone thought to polish obsidian
until it shone, who first stood by the lip of a lake?

Knelt on the bank of a still stretch of river, or stream?
Who leaned that tiny bit further forward,
peering into the watery depths at the kindred soul

rising up to greet them, whose image looked all too human?
Did that person keep it a secret, yet return to it
again and again, furtively? Did that person

recognise himself? Herself? Did fleshy folds of
face-down cheeks and jowls reflect a woefully distorted expression,
deep-socketed eyes staring back

as if from an underworld? A human face
rising from dark waters—more of a death mask
than the fabled beauty of the River God's son,

Narcissus, who, on reflection, fell so in love
with himself, with what he could never possess,
that he killed himself?

Or was it first a child, sent to keep an eye on the herd,
and while playing in the shallows of the local watering hole,
spent hours watching the muzzle of each animal

dip to meet its match: muzzle rising to muzzle
in a series of watery kisses? Did that child one day dare
to lower his or her small puzzled face and stare

in wonder at the meeting of another pair of fresh wet lips?
Who first tested the waters, whispering
maybe that's me ?

Foreign Mirrors

A new entry in her diary: *'Mother died yesterday.'*
She wanted to write something more. The telegram
had arrived that morning, her older sister,

stuck there in Athens, letting her know—the one left behind,
looking after their parents, now just Father.
Later, she'd write to her sister, commiserate.

Here she was, sent abroad to further her career—
a concert pianist, like her mother. Even if she had the money,
it would take four days to cross the Atlantic,

another two, by ship or train to Athens. She'd miss the funeral.
What should she do? Should she cover the mirrors
the way they did in Athens whenever a relative died?

But this was New York. Could evil spirits, the devil,
reach this far, pass through glass to trap her mother's soul,
enter foreign mirrors? She had no one whose answer she could trust.

She drifted in a kind of trance from room to room, staring into mirrors,
debating whether to drape each shimmering surface. Slowly,
she began to see a reflection of her mother

not as she'd left her, over three years ago, ageing, frail,
smiling at her daughter's promise to return within a year's time,
but as a young woman, thrilling audiences

with her dexterity and brilliance. She thought back
to her own childhood, her debut at Athens Conservatory
at nine years old—to why she was here.

The silvered glass would stay open to the hard winter light.
She folded away the cloths, gathered her things,
left the apartment, and walked across Central Park to her master class.

She played especially well that afternoon, to honour her mother's life—
her wish for her, the younger daughter,
'to fulfil your talent'. And let the devil take the hindmost, she said

to no one in particular as she made her way home.
This was a phrase she'd heard in an American radio play, and liked
the sound of it. She had no idea what it meant.

The Piano and the Violin

A SHORT STORY

'So we're talkin' three, four, faahv machines!' Carla thrust out her hand traffic cop-style, palm outward, fingers fully splayed.

Carla repeated the number with another swift extension of her long, lean arm, bringing her outstretched palm to within millimetres of Frosso's prominent Greek nose. 'Faahv, Miss Frosso!'

'Yes, well, then it is five.' Frosso tried not to flinch from the proximity of Carla's flesh. 'Here then are five quarters and five dimes.' She parcelled out the money ceremoniously from a tiny, imitation leather purse with its tarnished metal closure. 'And two dollars for the various dryers. The change machine downstairs will give you tokens. Is that clear?' Frosso placed the money into Carla's cupped hand, suppressing a shudder. Even the pink of this woman's palm was of a different hue to her own.

'Dried separately, too?' Carla sighed at the sheer waste of time and money. 'An' what about your skirt an' all those fancy tops over there?' Carla pointed to the piano bench. A plain navy cotton skirt, identical to the one Frosso was wearing, lay alongside an exotic pool of silky print blouses.

'I shall worry about the rest of these clothes.' Frosso positioned herself between Carla and the piano bench as if some unforeseen gesture of this agile black woman might suddenly spirit them away and deposit them into the laundry basket. Why was she allowing a black woman to do the laundry, if the mere sight of her skin was so upsetting?

But there was, Frosso reminded herself sternly, no other way. And we are all people of God, she muttered, the God, who had called her here from Athens. Here, to this enormous, bewildering country, to look after Aspasia, her suddenly widowed sister, who was not only difficult and did not love Jesus, but was ill, and could hardly walk.

Even with all the American conveniences—more than she ever imagined from the many books she'd read, the glossy magazines she'd gazed at over the decades—nonetheless, there was still so much to do each day.

Aspasia's daughter, Andrea, had moved to England so there was no help coming from that quarter. True, Andrea's brother lived nearby.

He and his wife certainly did their best. Money was no object! But she, Frosso, yes, she was the one in charge of her sister now. Aspasia had become her responsibility.

After a lifetime of living thousands of miles apart, God had given her the task of caring for her younger sister. However onerous it might be at times, I will have to learn to shoulder this burden.

'How is that, Miss Frosso?' 'You say you wanna shoulder the burden? Hey, I don't mind doing the laundry! It's my job! Just sayin' how easy it'd be to mix it all together—like one happy family!'

'No, no, Carla, I was talking to myself. You will do as I say. This is how we will handle the laundry.'

'One last thing, Miss Frosso—not to be disrespectful—but have you ever stuck your head inside one a those huge dryin' machines right after they stop spinning? Nothin' in this world could stay alive for two minutes in that heat. Like that TV ad says—kills all known germs dead!' Carla folded her arms resolutely, case concluded.

'Very well then, Carla. I shall go and do the laundry myself. I do not mind! I did it last week. You will be here vacuuming so Aspasia will not be left on her own.' Frosso moved purposefully past Carla to the laundry basket which was afloat with small plastic bags, each one knotted tightly at its throat.

'OK, OK, Miss Frosso. You win! I'll go get everything washed separately just the way you like it: your undies, Miss Spasia's undies, one kitchen towel, two bathroom towels, and a couple of sheets. That's the faahv machines, right?'

'Very good, Carla. Yes, we will see you later.'

'Each little load's gonna be twirlin' round on its own in all those big ole machines...'

'Yes, and if there are not five machines free, you may return here if you like. Naturally, you must bring the unwashed laundry upstairs with you. Do not leave it unattended. Someone may steal it. I am not saying that there are ladies in this beautiful building who like to steal, who are,' Frosso grabbed Carla's arm, intensifying her voice—'thiefs—but who knows? Someone else, perhaps from outside, a stranger! Not everyone, Carla, is a good person'. She released her hold on Carla's arm and smiled at her.

'Thieves, Frosso. Not thiefs!' Her sister's correction was issued from the depths of the sofa, at the far side of the living room.

'Yes, yes, Aspasia, all right. Theeeves. Thank you. My English is not as perfect as yours. So. Carla. Now you are ready to go? And you understand everything I am saying, yes?'

'Oh, I understand everything, Miss Frosso. Now you just stop worryin' about this subject and take care of your sister. I'm gonna grab hold of those machines one by one, 'till there's no machines left for anyone else's laundry today.'

Carla leant down and lifted the green plastic laundry basket, slotting it in one smooth movement under her long arm as neatly and easily as an athlete would a basketball. It was the lightest load she'd lifted in all the years she'd been working, and she began walking toward the front door which led out into the common hallway.

Frosso was close behind, seeing Carla to the elevator, when Aspasia's voice rang out from the apartment through the half-open door:

'Ridiculous! Come back here, both of you.' The strength of Aspasia's voice surprised them both. So full of scorn, it snagged the air between them. Frosso and Carla paused and stood for a moment, before walking back into the apartment.

'Five machines, Frosso! You make extra work for everyone. Carla! Don't listen to everything my sister says. She has such old-fashion ideas. She is not American like us.'

'Ah, I see,' said Frosso. She had dragged the laundry basket, and Carla with it, backward into the living room. 'Carla, now Mrs Dritsas will tell you how she would like you to do the laundry. I will take out my few things and wash them by hand. Put the basket down, please.'

Frosso began squeezing the various plastic bags to determine which ones held her things. With her bony fingers, she attempted to tear into the knotted plastic.

'Now, now, girls', sighed Carla. 'We been standin' here half an hour doin' nothin' but discussin' these poor clothes...'

Carla began to see her luxurious free time down in the blissful anonymity of the basement suddenly evaporating. Although Carla had initially thought it crazy, that laundry fetish of Frosso's to separate everything had begun to sound like a great idea after all. It would give her at least two full hours on her own, drifting in and out of the building, getting some fresh air, having a few smokes in the back parking lot where she couldn't be spotted from their front-facing windows.

'All your life you've spent in Athens, Frosso, without any children or even a husband. How can you know about washing machines and dryers?' Aspasia demanded. 'You think the other ladies do tiny little loads with one towel each?'

'And what do I care about these American ladies? They are not like me. Ach! Let them do whatever they want.'

'Imagine,' continued Aspasia seamlessly, 'you are asking Carla to use five machines to wash, and five to dry. Two, at the most! Whites and coloureds, and then, everything goes in the dryer. That's all. Finished, the discussion.'

The apartment went quiet. The strength of Aspasia's voice utterly contradicted her emaciated frame and seemed to derive solely from her head, which now seemed too large for her wasted body. Her complexion was marked more by age than illness, and her features resembled those of an old man's, with deeply socketed eyes, the same prominent nose as her sister's, and a huge sloping forehead. Her short, thick hair was white, starkly combed with a precise side parting. The muscles in her face were rigid from tension and the advancing stasis, or mask, characteristic of Parkinson's disease.

'Ach, ach, Aspasouli.' Frosso was defeated by the similar-looking plastic bags which she had knotted so efficiently, and which now would not yield their dirty secrets. She knelt among them, in her girlish white blouse and unseasonal cotton skirt. Her thin, curled, inexpertly dyed brown hair contrasted harshly with her chalk white complexion; she, who, like her sister, would never see seventy-five again, looked like a sickly child forced to play indoors, a lonely child who had lost the most important piece of her jig-saw puzzle, the one which would make sense of everything else. 'How unhappy you make me. Shall I go home then? Back to my home.'

Frosso stood up and smoothed her creased skirt. 'How I miss Greece. But it is the will of God for me to be here. Here, with my be-love-ed sister.' The adjective congealed on her tongue like cold honey. Frosso looked directly at Aspasia who showed no reaction, and then past her to the windows beyond the sofa where only sky and the tops of trees were visible, swaying in the Fall winds.

'Praise God and give me strength. Praise Jesus. I will do what he asks. My duty is here.'

Frosso returned her gaze to the laundry basket which she had emptied and began putting back the plastic bags, one by one, as carefully as if they were newly laid eggs. When she finished, she walked over to the sofa:

'Can't you see, Aspasia, that Carla is waiting to go and do as she is told.'

Frosso then turned to face the tall, patient, black woman: 'You see, Carla, you must do as you are told, and I must do as I am told'. Frosso's gaze shifted to the windows again, and the trees. 'But of course, only God can tell us what we must do, not what we want to do—but what we must do, if we listen. And of course, Aspasia does not listen to anyone. Not to me, not to Jesus, to no one.'

Frosso's eyes darted back to Aspasia, who was wearing a half-smile, as undecipherable as that of a Greek statue.

'You see, Carla? Aspasia is smiling, but she doesn't listen.' Frosso moved even closer to her sister. 'You are smiling, Aspasia. Good. Are you happy?'

Aspasia held her smile of bemused tolerance, but said nothing. It was difficult to tell whether the atrophied muscles were responsible for her mask-like expression, or whether it was by choice that she remained in that silent, unforthcoming, mildly-taunting pose.

'Ach! Now you do not want to talk. Now that I am talking to you, you Aspasouli mou, my little sister, you do not want to talk.'

After a moment, Frosso backed away, shrugging her birdlike shoulders in a hurt, resigned manner.

'Go, Carla. Do as Frosso tells you.' Aspasia's bored, imperious voice broke the silence. She dismissed them both as if she were royalty and the jesters had become tiresome, their antics repetitive. Frosso, taken by surprise, swivelled around to face her. Carla simply stared. Both women understood this was the final edict on the subject.

'Now no bickerin' while I'm gone, you two!' Carla wasn't going to miss this chance to make a move. She breathed an inner sigh of relief at the outcome—a surprise reversal—and although events had turned out in her favour, she couldn't really say which sister had won. Not that she gave a damn. So she smiled at each of them equally brightly, picked up the green plastic basket for the second time that morning and quickly slipped out of the apartment.

Carla pressed for the elevator, felt in the back pocket of her jeans for her cigarettes, and fingered her way into the pack. She could hardly wait to light up. Being cooped up in that atmosphere was hell. *If it wasn't for Miss Spasia's son and his wife I wouldn't stick at this job another minute.* She'd worked for that family for over ten years. When they asked her to help out here, just until they found another solution, Carla never thought twice. Now she was trapped. *America don't suit everybody. Maybe Miss Frosso will be headin' back to her homeland soon enough and leave us be.*

Carla kept eyeing the long corridor to make sure Miss Frosso didn't suddenly burst out of the apartment with yet another set of laundry rules. Carla thought about taking the stairs—but ten flights, double height ones, was a long way down. And those stairwells were a bit scary, even in a fancy building like this. And her being black. What if someone thought she was a burglar? Nervously, she lit up the cigarette just seconds before the elevator arrived, its doors opening to reveal an empty space. Nonetheless, she couldn't risk setting off the smoking alarm.

'Damn this no smoking business.' Carla delicately stubbed out her cigarette on the heel of her sneaker. When she was sure it was no longer smouldering, she placed it ever so gingerly among the plastic bags, swung the basket into the elevator and pressed Basement. She'd light up again there and finish it in peace.

* * *

'Frosso! Bring me my tea, please. I must take my medicine.'

'Yes, Aspasia, I am coming immediately.' Frosso hurried out of the corner of the kitchen where she had been sitting immersed in her Bible, and presented Aspasia with her half-finished, tepid cup of tea and a small cylindrical plastic container. 'Two pills, yes?' Frosso picked at the twist-off cap without success.

'Hurry, Frosso. It's one thirty. I should have taken my pills at twelve noon sharp. I fell asleep.'

'Ach, I am sorry, Aspasia. So whose fault is that? Mine? I cannot open this. Do you know how to open these tops?' Frosso brought the miniscule container closer to the window and tilted it to catch the light: 'Let me read this now, the instructions are here on the side. Why so small they are written?'

'The arrows, Frosso! You see the little arrows? Bring it to me.'

'Come here then, to the kitchen, Aspasia, and you can show me. You have your cane and your walker. Get a little exercise. It will do you good!' Frosso was twisting and twisting the top, searching for the matching arrows.

'How can you talk to me about getting exercise. Imagine! I have to take my pills now. Then we must eat lunch, immediately. Bring it to me, Frosso, I said.'

Aspasia was sitting upright on the luxurious cream sofa. Strategically-placed small cushions of every shape supported her neck, her arms, and helped to prop up her spine which was clenched like a fist, and had given her body the permanent curvature of a hunchback.

Her favourite green silk paisley blouse no longer fitted her properly, but was perfectly coordinated with her immaculate grey wool skirt. And her stockinged legs, bent at the knees, thin as two willow branches, hung over the sofa's edge, curving away from each other at the calves, meeting again at her thickly-soled flat shoes.

A cane and metal walker were stationed alongside the sofa to Aspasia's immediate left. On her right was an end-table littered with pads, pens, pencils, stamps, chequebooks, address books, the telephone, and now, her tea. The telephone cord ran diagonally past her elbow to the back wall, hemming her in.

'I did it! Yes, the arrows must meet! Two pills, then. Did you say two, Aspasia?' Frosso inquired as if this were a splendid tea party and she was merely confirming how many lumps of sugar her sister desired.

'Yes, yes, Frosso. You're losing your memory.' Aspasia held the tea with some difficulty in her right hand, which was the one that trembled, but not at this particular moment. With her left hand, she placed the two tiny pills on her tongue, took a quick swallow of the tepid tea and downed them both.

'Finish the tea, Aspasia. It's good for you. Chamomile.' Although they conversed in English, Frosso pronounced it with the soft, Greek caressing 'ch', and the wide smile of 'ee': Chamommeele.

'I don't want any more. Thank you, dear. Go and rest. Then we will have lunch. You look very tired.' Aspasia handed her the cup and leant her head back on the cushions.

'Tired? Yes, of course I'm tired. But I'm well, thank the Lord. I will sit and play a little piano. Could I do that?' Frosso stood patiently waiting for the reply, like a schoolgirl in front of the headmistress.

'Of course! Go ahead. Why do you ask me that?' Aspasia looked away, her eyes eventually focusing on the table alongside her. She reached over and fussed with a scrap of paper, a list of some sort. The audience was over.

'Very well then.' Frosso stalked off into the kitchen to deposit the still-unfinished cup of tea in the sink, and to put the vial of pills in its assigned bowl. 'I ask', Frosso said, loudly enough for her voice to carry into the living room, because this is your house, and not mine'. She rinsed the tea cup and put it in the dishwasher. 'In my house,' Frosso muttered, 'I can do whatever I want'.

Frosso returned to the living room and sat at the piano. It was a professional Steinway upright. Frosso knew that her sister had waited nearly her whole life to own this superior instrument, but Aspasia's Parkinson's disease had progressed to the point where she could no longer take pleasure in this, her most treasured possession.

There had been a year, perhaps two, when the Steinway was brand new, and the trembling of her hands had not been as pronounced as it now was; when other ailments had not yet entered her system to complicate things even further; when her fingers had been able to execute the difficult sonatas and scherzos with a semblance of her former brilliance. But this was before Frosso had moved here from Athens. Before Mr Dritsas had died, suddenly, of a heart attack.

'What shall I play, Aspasia?' Frosso was considering the various choices before her, handling the various fragile scores of music with great care. 'Do you remember how you used to play this Scriabin? And Mother, too. How she played!'

'Of course I remember,' replied her sister, matter-of-factly. 'You think I don't remember?' The sofa faced the piano. Aspasia was confronted with Frosso's back.

'Would you like to play it?' Frosso asked. 'I cannot. Scriabin is too difficult for me.'

'Play something else. Play the Beethoven.'

'Yes, all right. The Pathétique.' Frosso opened the thick, lime-green book of Beethoven Sonatas that had belonged to their mother, a concert pianist, leafing through the pages until she found the start of it. But instead of attacking the opening passage, Frosso suddenly turned away from the keys and half-twisted her body on the narrow black bench to look at her sister:

'Ach, Aspasia, how I wanted to learn the piano instead of the violin. I hated the violin. But no! You and Mother were always at the piano. And such talent. Two concert pianists. What could I do? I had no choice. I had to settle for the violin.'

'How you make these things up, Frosso.' Aspasia spoke without once glancing up from her scraps of paper. 'I don't remember that you ever wanted to learn the piano.' Her reply seemed absent-minded, yet laced with a sufficiently strong note of irritation to close off any further discussion.

'What is for lunch, Frosso?'

'Please, Aspasia! You do not remember? And you think it is I who am losing my memory! From a little girl I loved the piano, but it was not God's will.'

Frosso turned to face the keyboard, her arms outstretched as if she might embrace the entire instrument.

'And did you ask Mother?' Aspasia honoured her sister at last with her full attention.

Her tone was chiding, with a grace-note of urgency—as if Frosso had been forgetful not only as a child, but was, in fact, still that child, and must go immediately into the next room, find their all-comprehending mother and attempt to have this trifling misunderstanding corrected.

'Ask? What was the use of asking? You were the pianist. You were the gifted one, with the beautiful dresses.'

Frosso's thin, tired face was lost in rapture. 'You remember that dress you wore for the concert at the Athens Conservatory when Cousin George threw you the huge bouquet of flowers?' There was not a trace of envy now in her tone.

'Yes, I remember it. What I played. All those flowers, my beautiful dress. How very proud Mother was. I was nine.'

'And I was eleven.' Frosso sighed deeply, facing the Steinway. The room was silent. Aspasia watched as her sister at last placed both hands carefully in position above the keys and threw her birdlike shoulders forward in an effort to give her fingers as much strength as possible.

Frosso played the Sonata's entire first movement meticulously, and without too many errors, avoiding any show of bravura, concentrating instead on an even tempo which she could sustain throughout.

Every now and then her sister would call out 'B Flat' or whatever was the correct note. Not only did Aspasia know the piece as if she'd composed it, she had been born with the gift of perfect pitch, and like her mother, could detect a wrong note even when played within a complex chord. Neither Andrea nor her brother had inherited this.

Just as Frosso was about to press on with the dolorous, heart-rending second movement, the sisters heard the sound of the doorbell.

If only it were my Andrea, Aspasia thought. But she lives so far away now. Who knows when she will visit? It's probably José, finally showing up to repair the broken towel rail. Or Carla, needing a bit more change to finish the laundry.

Epilogue

The Long Now

i

Here, in the long now of this blazing day,
four black-faced clocks keep time.
I face the old coach house at quarter past nine,
its squat clock tower marking time, marking
time. I circle the four-faced crown.

I sip an espresso, and tap into Badakhshan:
six thousand years of mining in northeast
Afghanistan. Men breaking rock, releasing lapis lazuli—
prized for sacred amulets, scarabs and grave goods—
men crushing the lapis into a powder,
fine enough for a queen: Cleopatra's eye shadow.

ii

I've lost all track of time.
I pocket my pen and iPhone
and check my white-faced watch.
Its hands are clasped together in their ritual midnight prayer:
I pray for the long now
to continue for the next ten thousand years or so,
to the last syllable of recorded time.

In tonight's cooling air, four pairs of hands,
a fifth pair on my wrist, open out minutely
as if to welcome the small hours.

iii

Here, in the shadow of the tower,
I linger a while longer, imagining
first light, six thousand years ago. Tomorrow
and tomorrow and tomorrow, how many will I know?
I swam out into the river of minutes and days
seventy years ago, into the middle of the long now.

I count the years before me, consider those ahead.
Each year the swallows return, their song as old
as Africa. As old as Akrotiri. Tomorrow, will I walk
beneath a sky as blue as Cleopatra's eye shadow?
Blue as the lapis set in my silver ring?
Grave goods, grave goods. Tonight, I slip it off.

Notes

ABANDONED GARDENS
Kalos orisate! : Welcome.
krokalia: Small, often sharp, cobbled paving stones arranged in decorative geometric patterns, used both indoors and out.

AIVALI
'Aivali', the Greek name for this Anatolian harbour town was changed to the Turkish 'Ayvalik', after the so-called 'population exchange' in 1922.

ORNAMENT OF ASIA
In 1922, from the 11th-14th September, Smyrna was virtually destroyed by fire. This was the culmination of the ongoing, brutal conflict between the Anatolian Greeks and Kemal Attaturk's victorious army. Strabo, writing in the Augustan age, described Smyrna as the finest city in Asia, famous for its harbour, and as Homer's birthplace. Known as the Ornament of Asia, Smyrna rivalled ancient Ephesus.

FLAGS
Mahno no Varva Ino – Day of the Evil Spirit.

CASTLES IN THE AIR
'If you have built castles in the air, your work need not be lost; that is where they should be. Now put the foundation under them.'
                    —Henry David Thoreau (1817-1862)

CALLIGRAPHY
The quotation is from John Fowles in his novel *The Magus*.

MAEN EGLOS, LIZARD PENINSULA
Maen eglos: Cornish for rocks of the church.

EARTHSCAPES: THE LIZARD
Goon is Cornish for pony.

WIDE-EYED
Note: I owe my phrase 'quickened all into verb, / pure verb', to Seamus Heaney's closing line of 'Oysters': 'Might quicken me all into verb, pure verb'.

THE EMPEROR'S EXPERIMENT (II)
The unethical sensory deprivation led cultural historian Roger Shattuck to call it 'The Forbidden Experiment'.

EPILOGUE: THE LONG NOW

'The Long Now' is a term coined by Brian Eno, a founding member of The Long Now Foundation.

San Francisco-based, it is dedicated to long term thinking, stretching out what people consider as now. Brian Eno, on moving to New York City, realised that 'here' and 'now' referred to 'this room' and 'this five minutes' as opposed to the larger here, and longer now, that he was used to in England.

One of its projects, aimed to act 'as a balancing corrective to the short-sightedness' is to construct a 10,000-year clock powered by seasonal temperature changes, a mechanism 'which ticks once a year, bongs once a century, and the cuckoo comes out every millennium', an idea instigated by computer scientist Daniel Hillis.

Lightning Source UK Ltd.
Milton Keynes UK
UKOW03f0314260417
299885UK00002B/117/P